POSITIVE STEPS

Dealing with Differences

by Susan Martineau

with illustrations by Hel James

A⁺

Smart Apple Media

Published by Smart Apple Media
P.O. Box 3263, Mankato, Minnesota 56002

Printed in the United States of America at Corporate Graphics, in North Mankato, Minnesota.

Library of Congress Cataloging-in-Publication Data
Martineau, Susan.
 Dealing with differences / by Susan Martineau with illustrations by Hel James Smart.
    p. cm. -- (Positive steps)
 Includes index.
 ISBN 978-1-59920-492-5 (library binding)
 1. Social psychology--Juvenile literature. 2. Intergroup relations--Juvenile literature.
 3. Race relations--Juvenile literature. I. Title.
 HM1035.M37 2012
 305--dc22

                                                          2011011724

Created by Appleseed Editions. Ltd.
Designed and illustrated by Hel James
Edited by Mary-Jane Wilkins
Picture research by Su Alexander

Picture credits
Contents page Dick Luria/Thinkstock; 4t Stockbyte/Thinkstock, b BananaStock/ Thinkstock; 5 Stockbyte/Thinkstock; 6 AraBus/Shutterstock; 8 Phase4Photography/ Shutterstock; 9,10, 11, 12, 13 & 14t Thinkstock, b Jupiterimages/Thinkstock; 15 BananaStock/Thinkstock; 16t & br Thinkstock, bl Jack Hollingsworth/Thinkstock; 17t Hemera Technologies/Thinkstock, b Thinkstock; 18 Jupiterimages/Thinkstock; 19 Rohit Seth/Shutterstock; 20 Shutterstock; 21 Creatas Images/Thinkstock; 22 Digital Vision/Thinkstock; 23 Pixland/Thinkstock; 24 Jupiterimages/Thinkstock; 25t Benis Arapovic/Shutterstock, b Jupiterimages/Thinkstock; 26 Jupiterimages/Thinkstock; 26-27 background Thinkstock; 27 Jack Hollingsworth/Thinkstock; 28-29 Lakov Kalinin/ Shutterstock; 32 Darrin Klimek/Thinkstock
Cover: Mamahoohooba/Shutterstock

DAD0048
3-2011

9 8 7 6 5 4 3 2 1

Contents

It's fun to meet different people.

Everyone Is Different

Everyone is different. Imagine how boring it would be if we were all the same. Our differences make the world a wonderful, exciting place.

Our differences do not mean that some people are better than others. We are all just as important as each other, and we should feel proud of the way we are.

LET'S TALK ABOUT . . .

Think of all the ways people can be different. See if you can add more words to the list below. It might take a long time!

short

tall

old

young

dark-haired

light-haired

Don't Judge Too Soon

Sometimes we might decide whether we like someone or not from their **appearance** or the way they look. We cannot really know someone just by looking at them.

I don't like that new girl. She looks a bit weird.

But you haven't even spoken to her yet! She might be really nice.

We are judging too soon if we think someone is not nice just because they look a bit different from us or if they behave in a different way. This is called being **prejudiced**.

*Think about the ways
you and your friends are
different from each other.
Some differences are small
and some are large. None
of these differences stop
you from being friends
with each other.*

The Favorites Game

Sit next to someone you do not
normally sit with. Look at the person
and, without speaking to them, write
down three things about them:

- their favorite food
- their favorite TV show
- their favorite color

Now ask them and see if you are
right about them!

My favorite
color
is red.

Does he like
blue or red
best?

7

Be Yourself!

Rhiannon likes to be with her friends, but sometimes she does not really like the things they say about other people.

Rhiannon feels bad because she does not really agree with the others. She does not want to say what she thinks because she does not want to lose her friends.

LET'S TALK ABOUT . . .

Do you think it would be better if Rhiannon just said what she thought? Can you think of times when you have said or done things because you did not want to seem different from your friends? It is not always easy to speak up for yourself.

I like math!

I prefer English!

What can you do?

- Decide for yourself what you like and dislike.

- Have confidence in what you think and believe is right.

- Don't just follow the crowd.

- Remember that there is nothing wrong with being different.

- Be yourself!

I don't really like this TV show they all love.

Soccer for Everyone

Alice and Amber have always loved playing soccer, but the boys at school won't let them play because they are girls. Even the other girls think they should be playing different games with them instead.

Boys and girls are different, but they should be given the same, or **equal**, chance to do things. When someone is not allowed to do something because they are a girl or a boy, it is called **discrimination**.

Girls aren't good at soccer! You can't play.

LET'S TALK ABOUT . . .

Can you think of other ways that girls or boys are sometimes treated differently? What do you think of this?

Ballet and dance are lots of fun for both boys and girls.

Let us show you how good we are!

Word Power

Get into pairs and talk about how you might persuade the boys to let Amber and Alice play soccer. Think of what you might say.

Dealing with Racism

Charlie has made friends with a new boy named Jamal, but some of the other kids are saying horrible things about him. Charlie is writing to his friend Ben about it.

When someone is teased or bullied because they come from a different country or their skin is a different color, it is called **racism**. Racism is a kind of discrimination. We should remember that the important thing is the kind of person someone is. It does not matter where they come from or what they look like.

Hi Ben,

I hope you are having fun in your new school. There is a new boy here named Jamal. I like him but some of the others say horrible things about him because he has dark skin. They're mean.

See you soon.

Charlie

- A **race** is a group of people who come from the same part of the world and have the same skin color and type of hair.

- A racist is someone who treats other people unfairly because they belong to a different race.

- Racism is against the law.

What can you do?

- Tell anyone who makes racist remarks that it is wrong.

- Don't laugh when someone makes racist jokes.

- Don't tell racist jokes.

- Comfort anyone you see being bullied like this.

- Tell a grown-up if the racist bullying does not stop or you are bullied in this way.

Understanding Each Other

There are many different countries and races of people in our fascinating world. People speak many different languages. Some people can speak more than one language.

I speak Urdu.

When people leave their own country to live somewhere else, they bring their language with them as well as their different **customs** or ways of doing things. We can learn a lot about the world by getting to know them.

I speak Spanish.

I speak Chinese and English.

What can you do?

- Be welcoming to people from other countries.

- If they cannot speak your language, you can help them learn.

- Learn some of their language too!

Reading stories is a good way to learn a language.

un   ek

yí   uno

1   one

Language Challenge!

You or your friends may come from another country. Your classmates may know lots of different languages. Find out how many languages you know altogether. Then see if you can learn how to count to ten in each one. You could even learn a song in a different language too.

deux   do

èr   dos

2   two

3   teen   tres

trois   sān   three

What Do You Believe?

There are many different **religions** in the world. A religion is what people believe about God or gods and how they pray or **worship**.

We should **respect** the **beliefs** and religions of other people. They should also respect ours. It is fun to find out about other people's religions and their festivals or celebrations. Sometimes people wear different clothes or eat different food because of their religion.

Muslims pray five times a day.

Christians believe in one God and his son Jesus Christ.

Hindus believe in many gods.

LET'S TALK ABOUT . . .

Can you think of some different religions? Look below for some ideas. What religions do you and your friends follow? Not everyone follows a religion.

I'm not sure what I believe yet.

Christianity

Christmas

Time to Celebrate

Choose a religious festival or celebration. Here are some ideas to get you started, but there are many, many others to discover. Find out about the story behind the festival and how it is **celebrated**.

Judaism

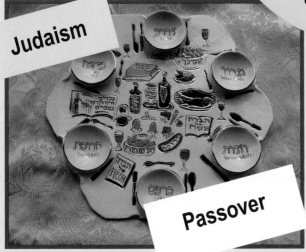

Passover

Diwali

Hinduism

Try Something Different

People around the world eat all kinds of different and delicious food. Perhaps you have a friend from another country where the food is different from yours.

Sometimes people eat certain food because of their religion or what they believe. They might be vegetarian. This means they do not eat meat. Some people eat with knives and forks and others use chopsticks or their hands.

Sook Ling eats noodles with chopsticks.

Jack loves hotdogs.

Anna's favorite food is fajitas.

I love my mom's spicy curries.

Ask your friends what their favorite food is. Maybe their family eats different food from yours. If you are invited to eat with them, always try the food even if it is not the same as yours.

A World Menu

Ask everyone in your class to name a dish from another country. It could be one that they eat at home. Draw a menu of all the different types of dishes.

Our Menu

chapattis

spaghetti

pita bread sandwich

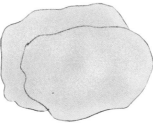

chilli con carne

hamburger

Chinese stir-fried rice

pizza

Thai curry and rice

I Can Do That!

Dan has impaired vision. This is a **disability** which means he cannot see very well. When he goes out, he uses a white cane to help him check where things are.

Dan has lots of other things to help him in class, but he knows he can always ask his friends to help too. If someone has a disability, this does not mean they cannot join in with everyone else.

Big print on a yellow screen makes it easier to see words on the computer.

My favorite sport is swimming.

Dan's talking watch tells him the time.

Respecting Older People

Sometimes older people seem to have different ways of doing things. We find it hard to imagine that they were once the same age as we are, but old and young people can learn from each other.

Older people have seen and done many things. We can learn lots from listening to them and their stories about life when they were young. We can also help them if they find some things hard to do as they get older.

I'm showing Grandma how to use our computer.

My grandpa tells me great stories about when he was young.

What can you do?
- Listen and learn from older people.

- Always be **polite** and respectful.

- Try and help older people if they are sick or disabled.

Looking Back
Imagine you are 80 years old. Think about some of the amazing inventions of the past 80 years. Then come back to the present and imagine what might be invented in the future during your lifetime.

dishwasher

computers

cell phones

color television

23

Welcoming New People

Aisha and her family had to leave their country because it was too dangerous for them to stay there. She is making friends at her new school but it is hard for her.

Aisha can't speak much English yet.

We're helping her.

LET'S TALK ABOUT . . .

How do you think Aisha must feel? She had to leave behind all her old friends and some of her family.

scared

lonely

sad

confused

We like helping Aisha learn English.

My new friends are fun.

What can you do?

- Be welcoming and kind to children like Aisha.

- Never tease them if they cannot **understand** you.

- Imagine how you would feel if you were Aisha.

Friends Around the World

We can learn about different countries and how people live in them by writing letters or e-mails to a pen pal from another part of the world.

E-mails are easy to send, but letters are fun as you see the different stamps from other countries. Always check with a grown-up before e-mailing or writing to a new friend.

Dear Will,

My name is Paulina and I live in Hamburg, Germany. I am learning English at school . . .

Dear Paulina,

Thanks for your letter. Can you tell me more about Germany? What are your hobbies?

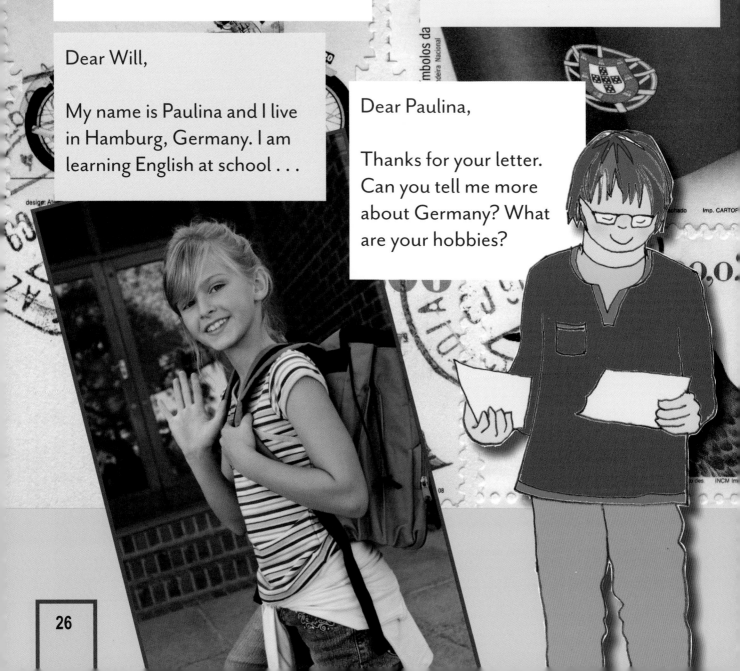

Hi Tyson,

What is it like living in New York City? I have only seen it in the movies. Do you play baseball or basketball? I love playing soccer.

Hi Robbie,

I guess my favorite sport is baseball. Do you play that in England?

Getting in Touch

Ask your teacher if your class could write to some children in another country. Think of some good questions to ask. Maybe you could have a special board in the classroom to display letters and photos.

Celebrating Differences

We can enjoy finding out about people who are different from us. Differences are not something to be afraid of or to dislike. The more we understand about other people, the better we get along with each other.

The important thing about someone is the kind of person they are inside and not what they look like on the outside. We are all equal, no matter where we come from, which language we speak, what clothes we wear, or what we believe.

What can you do?

Look at the Glossary on pages 30–31 to make sure you understand what they mean. Write some sentences using them. You could work in pairs and make some drawings to go with them.

All the bold words are explained on pages 30–31.

Be welcoming to people from other countries.

Make a difference. Show others you are not prejudiced.

Stick up for what you know is right, and be proud to be yourself.

Glossary

appearance
what someone looks like

belief
what someone believes

celebrate
to do something special or enjoyable on an important day

custom
a set way of doing something

disability
not able to use a part of your body properly because of illness or an injury

discrimination
treating someone unfairly or differently because of their race, sex, religion, or disability

equal
the same as each other

polite
having good manners

prejudiced
thinking that someone is not equal or the same just because they are different

race
a group of people who come from the same part of the world and have the same skin color and type of hair

racism

treating people unfairly because they come from a different race

religion

what people believe about God or gods and how they pray or worship

respect

being careful about the way you treat someone; showing you care about their feelings

understand

to know about something and what it means

worship

to show how much you love your God or gods

Web Sites

CDC – Kids Quest - Home
http://www.cdc.gov/ncbddd/kids/index.html

The More You Know – Diversity/Anti-Prejudice
http://www.themoreyouknow.com/for-kids/
diversity-anti-prejudice.shtml

URI Kids: World Religions
http://www.uri.org/kids/world.htm

I like getting to know other people.

Index

Respect everyone, whoever they are.